Ronnie Smith

RONNIE SMITH

MIRACLES

A PRODIGAL CHILD OF GOD

Copyright © 2020 by Ronnie Smith

ISBN: 9798655234178

All rights reserved. No part of this book may be reproduced or transmitted in any form or by any means, electronic or mechanical, including photocopying, recording, or by any information storage and retrieval system, without permission in writing from the copyright owner.

First Printing: August 2020

Manufactured and Printed in the United States

RAINBOW ROOM PUBLISHING
www.rainbowroompublishing.com

Ronnie Smith

Ronnie Smith

Table of Contents

Special Thanks..vii
Acknowledgements..ix
My Purpose...xii
Chapter 1..2
Chapter 2..22
Chapter 3..34
Chapter 4..38
Chapter 5..48
Chapter 6..60
Chapter 7..86
Chapter 8..94
Chapter 9..106
Chapter 10..112
Chapter 11..124
Chapter 12..136
Testimony...146
Reader Reviews...149

Special Thanks

To Charles Jones, who first inspired me to tell my story. He passed away since then, but he would always call me a miracle. That inspires my book title. He was a father, brother, mentor, and friend. He was on the hiring committee that first hired me as a personal assistant with the United States Post Office. He was also a tremendous help to me as I took guardianship of my younger sister while I was facing addiction to alcohol and drugs. May you rest in peace.

Much love,
Your Miracle.

Miracles

To Eleanor (Pat) Simpson, who was also a mother, friend, mentor, and a God sent angel in my life. She took me into her home and out of total self-destruction and depression, making me a part of her family. I became her Son and her children, Gwen and Tammy, became my sisters. Thank you to your entire family for your love and acceptance.

Your Prodigal Son.

ACKNOWLEDGEMENTS

Post Office Section 6 managers Solomon Sconiers and Donald Clark who without their caring, understanding, allowing me to go to rehabilitation and return to my position, I possibly would not have retired and be writing my story now.

My other managers Karen Washington, Loretta Wilkins, Jeanette Drain-Lake, Rosetta Johnson- Berry, Ms. Spinks, John L. Richardson, and JoAnn Clay. Thanks for your understanding and guidance through several personal health issues.

Rachell, my cyber navigator at Edgewater Library for your computer skills in preparation for completing my book.

Leonard and Patty Heidelburg for actually being the first to plant the seed in my mind to tell my story.

Thank you to my primary physician, Dr. Edwin J. Smolevitz from North Shore University Health System for your caring of me for over thirty years, not only as my Doctor, but you gave so much of your time and your heart as a mentor, adviser, therapist, caretaker and friend.

Thank you Deacon David Morris of Uptown Baptist Church for taking me under your wing and guiding me with your spiritual knowledge as a mentor, big brother, and friend.

Also a special thanks and acknowledgment to Eddie S. Pierce for his professionalism and guidance in editing, formatting, book cover design, publishing, distributing and marketing my memoir through the excellent services of his publishing company, Rainbow Room Publishing.

All thanks and gratitude to Jesus Christ my Lord and Savior.

Ronnie Smith

My Purpose

My purpose for sharing my life's journey is to help and show others like me that they, too, can overcome their adversities, struggles, trials, and tribulations. That they can know peace and joy. My story is an autobiography about my personal adventures, trials, and tribulations, a dysfunctional life while growing up a homosexual with inner fears, worry, stress, and low self-esteem. With no guidance, confused as a person but not a fight with society as many LGBTQ writers express, but more of a struggle within myself. Not so much in appearance as a gay man in public but still hiding and living in the closet. Although visible to some people, my real character did show in my younger years, but I did face a lot of personal criticism and bullying. Maybe I was as insecure as I thought. I was too busy fighting my depression.

So basically, that is what my story is about. My growth and ambition to help someone like me growing up with the same struggles. To encourage them to rise up with self-love and self-acceptance in a problematic world of prejudice and judgmental attitudes toward others different from them. To inspire them to push through their adversities. That you don't have to live with low self-esteem, fears, and worries. Especially those who aren't accepted by people in a world where judgment and criticism strongly exist towards the LGBT community.

This should be a lesson for all to learn about acceptance in our ever-changing society. That you can overcome sickness, sadness, and all evil that comes upon you and learn to trust and believe that Jesus is your Lord and Savior. As God shows us in the Bible, when he performed miracles by healing and saving people, he can also keep you if you believe and allow him in your heart. You can also receive blessings just as the prodigal child of the Gospel of Luke 15:11-32.

Ronnie Smith

In closing, maintaining a humble and caring heart after years of hurt, pain, loneliness, disappointments, and low self-esteem. After hitting rock bottom, then receiving blessings and mercy from Jesus, my Lord, and Savior to rise up with joy and happiness is quite a blessing.

A Prodigal Child of God,

Ronnie Smith

Ronnie Smith

CHAPTER 1

1953 – 1963

Bobbie Smith

Ronnie Smith

I was born December 13th, 1953, in Chicago, IL, at the Cook County Hospital. My mother's name was Bobbie Smith, and my father's name was Robert Blair. They are now deceased. Mom died 37 years ago. My dad passed only a few years ago, around 2011. My mom and dad never lived together because he was already married when they met. I lived with my mom for the first five or six years of my life.

I don't remember my dad, except only a few visits when he came around from time to time. I know that he was a friend of my Uncle Sam, who was married to my mom's sister called Honnie but, her real name was Velma. I grew up with her twelve children, who I still consider my siblings rather than cousins because we lived together. After my first five or six years, I lived with my Aunt Maud and Uncle GaGa on Larrabee Street.

Further down on Larrabee, my uncle owned a barbershop and restaurant. They took me because my mother wasn't able to take care of me. I think she had relationship problems and dealt with alcoholism. She wasn't very stable, and living with them was best for me. My mom already had two children that she left in Oak Grove, LA, with her grandmother. When she came back to Chicago years later, my sister's father took her to Colorado from Louisiana, and we were all separated. My brother remained in Louisiana with our great grandmother.

I feel that I had the most wonderful accepting mother in the world. She always showed me love and understanding of all that I was and wanted to be. I really had no relationship with my father, but I learned that he also had two other gay children. He said he loved me, but for some reason, I never believed it or *felt* his true love. Probably because he was never there after abandoning my mother for his traditional legal family.

My mom always told me to just love him as a friend. I will never forget those words. I truly believe those words helped me to stay the loving, forgiving, and understanding person that I am (most of the time). Trying not to blame other people. We all make mistakes, and through God's grace and mercy, we are ALL forgiven.

    I remember my mother's funeral. I road with my father, but he didn't want to get out of the car to see her being put in the ground. Since I never really knew my father or any of his ways, I wondered why he didn't want to get out of the car either. Maybe he was afraid. I stayed in the car with him. Maybe, I was scared because I was feeling his fears. Years later, I learned through other family members, that after my mom found out he was married with children, she began to drink heavily. I think maybe she drank to hide her hurt.

    I learned later that he had lots of women at his funeral from his other children. They joked and said, "Yeah, Papa was a rolling stone!"

    I saw my siblings maybe once or twice in my life at one of his other lady's homes on the West Side. The closest I ever felt around him was at his birthday party while he was with living with another woman. She had one child, a girl, who might be my sister.

I'm not sure. Also there was a women named Gloria. I spent some time with her and her two kids. I kept in touch with them until one day I had a party and invited them. They were turned off, after realizing I was gay. *Oh well!*

Another situation that sticks in my mind is my mom's kind and grateful spirit. When we know God is in our hearts and being a righteous and God-fearing person, the devil will always attempt to strike. I was nervous even more with hurt and pain in my heart from the death of my mom. At her funeral, my cousin Tina, the same one that took my sister, saw me putting a Bible in my mom's casket. Often my mom gave me scriptures from that Bible to read, or she would circle them for me. Tina took it out of the coffin. I wanted my mom to have a part of me, but I listened to Tina instead of myself, like my mom would have wanted me. I regret doing that. It still hurts me in my heart today.

My dad had a daughter, Wanda. I love her, but I don't understand her way of showing love to me. She made a meaningful statement about Daddy having all these gay kids. I wondered if that was some anger that she held. I don't know if it was held in anger from living with my partner and me. We asked her to move for personal reasons. I wanted to ask her about that for so long. However, we only express love on the phone during the holidays. I love you, Wanda, but I was just confused.

Robert Blair's Children

Before all of that, my mom and I lived on the first floor at Larrabee and North Avenue. My mom's sister Honnie and her husband, my Uncle Sam, lived upstairs from us. During this time, my mom became depressed and began to develop a drinking problem due to my father's infidelity. I have some memories of my time on Larrabee. Like when I was four or five and starting school. I remember the first church I attended was across the street on Larrabee Street. During those years, my neighborhood was racially mixed. I remember it having several races and many nationalities.

I later lived with my great aunt Maud on Larrabee and Clybourn not far from Cooley High School and Oscar-Meyer hot dog factory and a chocolate factory, always smelling chocolate. After about a year, we had to move because the city was preparing to build the Cabrini Green Projects. We later moved further up on Clybourn, near Ogden Street. My cousins would spend the weekends with me. It was like having brothers and sisters around me because I had no other siblings around.

One of the worst experiences of my life was attending Cooley Upper-Grade Center. It had grades seven thru twelve and was quite a transition for me coming from an all-white school to an all-Black school. Not putting my race down but as a non-violent mild-mannered person this change caused an unforgettable feeling of fear and anxiety each day. I remember receiving threats from a few bullies, but I also remember a few good friends. We would always go to Sammy's Hot Dog stand for lunch

My aunt also continued to drink. She said it was only beer, but some of my cousins said it was wine or something harder. Sometime later, my mom left and went away with her own drinking problem. Life was quite stressful for me at that time. Especially without having my siblings living with me. Sometimes my uncle's barbershop customers would bring their kids to the house, and I played with them. They were always boys. I remember playing what I called Chu Chu Train. We would all make a train holding on to each other and move around like a train. It sticks to my mind because I feel this was the beginning of my homosexuality.

My aunt would act a fool while customers were there. Cursing and slamming doors, angry with my uncle. I would just sit in my chair and watch TV. I'll always remember that chair; it was extremely comfortable. It was an antique chair in the corner of our front room with a partition that separated the living room from where I was watching television from my aunt's bedroom. My uncle's bedroom was a small space near our dining room and kitchen

I remember my father bringing me my first tricycle. He brought it to me because he lived with his wife and their children that I didn't know about at that point. I think the bike was the only thing he has ever done for me. That is still very hard for me to accept and later in my life caused me many problems mentally. My mom always told me to just to be his friend and not to be angry with him.

Living with my cousins was good. I guess you could say it was a blessing for me and a chance to have a "normal" life with a mother and a father. Even then, I was a bit sad and lonely because I missed living with my mom. Sometimes Ronald and James, who were the same age as me, would come to spend the weekend with me. Later Darrell and Timothy came as well. Then Diane stayed with us for a while. We had lots of fun together.

My uncle and aunt took excellent care of me. They had a restaurant with plenty of good ice cream and toys. We always had lots of dogs. Dobermans, named Trigger and Lady that repeatedly had lots of puppies. I remember I would often cry at night for my mother, and my aunt would always give me warm milk to help me sleep.

At that time, my cousin and I attended LaSalle Elementary School. The majority of my classmates were white kids, and Ronald, my cousin, and I were in the same class for six years. We were the only black boys in those classes. I remember our kindergarten teacher, Ms. Honky. Yes that was her actual name. From the first grade to sixth, I remember my cousin didn't talk to me very much. I guess that was just his way because he still doesn't speak to me very much.

I know I began school living with my mother, but I don't remember at what exact grade my aunt took me. I believe it was going into the seventh grade because I did attend Cooley School which was closer to her house. I vividly remember my Aunt Maud bringing me a coat and walking me home with her.

This was probably the beginning of loneliness and insecurity that would challenge me for years to come. My aunt took me to LaSalle School every morning until the sixth grade. At the age of about ten years old, I still lived with my aunt on Larrabee Street and Clybourn. I was transferred to Cooley Upper-Grade Center for 7th grade. Then we moved to another spot on Clybourn

My uncle bought a building on Clybourn Street, where we no longer owned the restaurant. The first floor was a storefront where we kept the storage and our dogs. My uncle also had a barbershop upstairs in the rear of the long hallway, separate from our apartment. The dogs had a homemade living quarter/doghouse in the corner of that long hallway, near the barbershop. My chores were to clean the barbershop floors, hallways, and the dog house. My cousin, Ronald, and I would get oil for our neighbors, to go make money.

I remember having a problem one day with this guy named Thomas that my cousin James knew. They were around the same age and went to school together or something. He lived around the corner, and every time we went to get the oil, Thomas would try to pick a fight with me. I remember now that was the beginning of how I became timid. I would be afraid because I wasn't used to fighting. I remember walking with the oil tins, and Ronald was never scared. During this time, many people had oil heaters, but we also had a coal and wood-burning heater to keep warm.

I had my own bedroom, and Darrell would come by to keep me company and sleep in my room. One day Levell, my cousin, came to stay with us. He got my room, and I moved to the middle room, which previously was my uncle's bedroom. My uncle's niece, Bessie Lee, stayed with us too. I remember her very well because she treated me nice and took me to see Martha & the Vandellas down the street. This area was close to the Cabrini Green Housing Projects that were being built.

My uncle bought me a 10-speed bike and a guitar. I was too small to ride the bike at first, but I later learned. However, I never got a chance to play the guitar because someone stole it during our next move. I've always regretted that. I wish I could play the guitar. I probably would have a different life. Possibly a more musical life. I was quite sad when my guitar was stolen because I did like music and singing and humming songs to myself. That still bothers me today. I often think of buying a guitar and taking guitar lessons. I feel I made a mistake by not trying to learn to play it. My uncle was trying to help my future, for which I am so grateful. He was trying to be a father. The bike gave me a chance to get away from the house and be with my cousins to ease the loneliness. They made me feel good but, I missed my mom.

That bike became a better friend than those pet dogs. I used to ride down Clybourn to my cousin's house on Weed Street. It wasn't far, just three or four blocks away. You could see their house from ours because there was a big ole plot of empty land between us. It was fun, lots of fun. This was during the early 60s, and I have terrific memories of Weed Street. It was like having our very own neighborhood with six or seven houses on one side of the street. On the other was the old folks' home project.

We used to play touch football in the grass, and I was kind of good. Although I've never been good at sports, I think I got many compliments when playing football. I guess I was kind of athletic. That was the last time I actually had fun with my male cousins. Playing sports. Except for the times, they played softball with other boys. Then I usually jumped rope or something with the girls.

I liked to do a lot of girly things. I knew I was gay then. I played hopscotch, Double Dutch, and jacks. My cousins were my brothers and sisters. I know my uncle was a hunter because he had a lot of hunting dogs. He'd always go and bring back rabbits and squirrels for meals. We also had some chickens in the backyard. My uncle would have live chickens and breed them too. I remember him ringing their necks sometimes.

I also went to school with this guy named Norman. He went hunting with my uncle and always wondered why I never went with them. His own sons didn't go either. I liked Norman a little bit. Honestly, I didn't know if I was gay or not back then. I mean, I did *know* I was, but, at any rate, I now wish I had taken that opportunity to learn more. I didn't show that I was gay. Even to this day, I'm not a person that looks gay. Don't get me wrong, I'm not hiding it. I'm totally out of the closet.

Anyway, those were some good days there, especially lots of fun on that front porch. There were always plenty of friends from the neighborhood. I would go through the alley and follow the elevated train tracks of the "El" known today as the Brown Line from Weed Street to North Avenue.

On the other side of us was Shirley Powell and her little sister, Debbie's house. They had a large vicious dog. Next to them was my old friend, Gene Martin, who is still my friend today. We are very close, and he is close to my family. We were in the same graduating class in high school and continued to live by each other on the North Side. He was very close to my family and me, especially. Gene was like a brother to me. I remember his mother, Juanita, his uncle Herb and his sister Lisa.

Gene, Ronald, and I often went to Cubs Park, Wrigley Field, and made some money shining shoes with our homemade shoe-shining box. The three of us often visited Riverview, the amusement park on the North Side, near Belmont Avenue. Riverview was such a fantastic amusement park. I think it was located around Belmont and Western Avenue. I had great memories for some poor black kids growing up on the Northside of Chicago. North Avenue Beach is the best from my childhood.

We would walk there to swim and play with other kids and sometimes to the movie theater in Old Town. Once we dressed up for Easter Sunday and went to the movies for ten cents. We had the penny candy store on North Avenue, known as Ms. Dones' Candy Store. We had so many great things to do and lots of candy for one penny. It was heaven to us.

Like I said earlier, I've been gay since I was 5 years old. When it came to my sexuality, I was afraid and confused, especially in light of some sexual activity with girls and being raped by an older woman while sleeping in my Godmother's bed in my teenage years. An awful experience I was too ashamed and confused to tell anyone.

One thing about my family is that they didn't criticize me. Not in front of my face, at least. I knew they knew I was gay, but they never pushed or rubbed that in my face. I do wish somebody talked to me about *that*. I never had anyone teach me about sex between a girl and a boy. No one *ever!*

Ronnie Smith

As an adult, I later realized that I missed going to sex education because I didn't want to go to gym class. Gym meant going swimming and go swimming meant getting naked with boys. I was very self-conscious of myself back then and very nervous about being around so many nude boys because I knew I was gay. I almost did not graduate because I did not want to be naked around so many boys while in the locker room or swimming naked showing them my private parts. I had to write an essay for the gym teacher to pass. What a blessing that was. God knew my heart.

As a result, I always had a desire to reach out to strange men around who I felt more comfortable and protected, which led to homosexual activity. With many men, in those days expressing homosexual feelings publicly wasn't permitted. Most boys my age grew up, as we say, in the closet. This added to my lack of self-esteem.

So I had several so-called friends, some dysfunctional family members, and several sexual conflicts. It was an unbelievably stressful time for a child.

We had other friends that lived around us. My first girlfriend, Vicky, lived a few houses down from us. I remember her mother, father, and sister, who was gay, I believe. She had a friend, a guy who was gay but I can't remember his name. This was all a very memorable and important time in my growing period. I was about ten or eleven.

Ronnie Smith

CHAPTER 2

1963 – 1968

"The Lord is my shepherd; I shall not want. He maketh me to lie down in green pastures: he leadeth me beside the still waters. He restoreth my soul: he leadeth me in the paths of righteousness for his name's sake. Yea, though I walk through the valley of the shadow of death, I will fear no evil: for thou art with me; thy rod and thy staff they comfort me. Thou preparest a table before me in the presence of mine enemies: thou anointest my head with oil; my cup runneth over. Surely goodness and mercy shall follow me all the days of my life: and I will dwell in the house of the Lord forever."
Psalm 23 King James Version (KJV)

Ronnie Smith

I remember the assassination of President John F. Kennedy in 1963. I was about nine or ten years old. There were lots of other people around Weed Street. It was like our own little neighborhood. We were let out of school early, and everybody ran home to watch it on television. It was a very sad day for our country.

There were only black people around Weed Street, Clybourn, Halsted, and North Avenue with the old folks' home across the street. Sharon and Coretta were sisters, and we would all hang out at their house. They had a basement apartment, and we would have twenty-five cent parties, known as Quarter Parties. Everyone would come. I had an attraction to Sharon, but I was too shy and timid to tell her my feelings. She started going with Eddie; he had a sister, Edna, and another sister Emma. Some other people were Erma Young and her family. The Flakes Family. Big Will and his brothers had a band that performed Temptation songs.

I'll always remember the house. We didn't have a lot of money or good-looking furniture. I say we because I was actually with my Aunt Maud and her husband, Uncle GaGa, but I always saw Honnie and Sam as my mom and dad. I spent many nights at their house as I could get away with. I had so many good memories on Weed Street. My uncle would always take us to the drive-in. I was just like their son when we gathered in their station wagon.

Another significant memory was the assassination of Dr. Martin Luther King Jr. I remember the anger that people were expressing, fires being set and the looting of many stores by our house on Weed Street near North Avenue. People were told to stay in our homes. To this day, I am very proud of his fight for freedom for all.

Eventually, we moved to 906 Willow. This was on the North Side in the Lincoln Park area. I was in the eighth grade, attending a new school in a different neighborhood when my aunt and uncle's separation started. This was when I started a job at Pete's Grocery Store. I wanted to try to support myself. Later, I worked at Red Goose Shoe Store on West North Avenue. This money put me through high school.

During that time, there was more dysfunction in my life. I was dealing with some anger from my aunt due to the changes in her life. I spent as much time as I could with the Gates family, and my cousins. They lived on Weed Street. When my cousins moved to the West Side, I ended up moving in with them.

Close to my graduation time from Waller High School, I couldn't stay with my mom on the South Side anymore, so I moved back to Aunt Honnie's. All this moving back and forth, with no parental structure male or female, created my need for a father figure and a search for male guidance.

I also remember confessing to a close school friend and neighborhood buddy, Robert Smith, after many years of friendship, that I was gay. He told me, "Are you CRAZY? Why do you think we didn't know that? We ALL knew that. You were one of our best friends. John T, Cletus and I talked about that all the time. It didn't matter to us. We all loved you."

This was all new to me, and it felt nice to make friends in a new area. I got to attend eighth grade at Arnold School. What a change from Cooley High Upgrade Center. I really liked the relocation and the neighborhood better than Weed Street. We lived in a two-story building. Our downstairs neighbors were the Gates, and I later became very close to them. Just like the other two apartments, we had the dogs and the barbershop.

I've never been an outgoing person. I was always a shy, quiet, and fearful person. When I was younger, I had little social growth, and at that time, I still had a long way to go with accepting myself. Not that I got much criticism from those around me. I just had problems with accepting me, Ronnie. I never really hung out much. I just went to school, played on the block on Willow, sit on Jap's porch, or went to Tootie's house with Gene and Bear.

Ronnie Smith

Gene Martin (friend), Linda Henry (cousin)

with Ronnie Smith

Gene and I even today talk about old times on Willow Street. Most guys hung at Clybourn Park to play ball. I would often spend nights at my cousin's house, or Gene would come over. Sometimes he would spend the night and keep me company when I was living with my aunt on Willow Street. He moved into my area on Bissell, I think. I remember having radio battles with him. He had the Temptations, and I had The Miracles, our music battles were always lots of fun. I never was much of a Sportsman, I remember Gene always talking about being a Sportscaster on the radio and TV. When we began high school, we didn't spend as much time together but remained friends, and so did our families. I don't remember having any classes with him. Maybe Gym, but I still didn't get as involved as he did.

I was very insecure back then. I am happy to say that I did have some experience with girls later. There was Shirley, Grace, Linda, and Arlisha. Then, there was this other girl that Freddie, my roommate, and I had a sexual experience with. Although I experienced intimacy with some of those women, it never stopped me from being a gay man.

It really was a blessing not to go to Cooley High anymore. That year at Cooley was horrible, and mostly all the black kids were violent. There were always fights from the first day. Coming from mostly white LaSalle was a major transition for me; it was quite a change. The kids at Cooley High were scary. Our neighborhood was always about 80% black.

Ronnie Smith

After about six months on Willow Street, my Uncle GaGa decided to leave my Aunt Maud. After he left, it was just her, the dogs and me. During that time, I started visiting my mom on the South Side. She lived on 39th and Indiana. There were other places I visited her, too. I took the El to her; it was called the A & B Line back then. Now known as the Green Line. I mostly looked out the window watching the city and staying out of trouble with the criminals on the train.

I began to hang around the Gates family, Jeanette, and Frank, and their children Peter, Gloria, DeeDee, K.O., Lucille, and Van. Peter and Gloria, were about the same age as me, so Gloria and I went to the same school, Arnold High Upper Grade Center School. I ended up becoming close friends with the whole family. Jeanette's sisters and brothers also lived in the neighborhood. Her sister Pat eventually became my Godmother, and her kids Tammy and Gwen became my sisters. I lived with them for a few years on the South Side.

I would hang with Peter all the time. I remember us going to the corner restaurant and playing the jukebox. It cost a dime back in 1967-68. Some of my more memorable times was hanging out at Peter's girlfriend, Doris' house. She lived on Fremont and had a sister named Silvia, whom I liked a little but was too shy to go for it. Or maybe I just wasn't attracted enough to girls? As time went by, I ended up taking this girl named Linda up to our house and lost my virginity to her in the barbershop under the chair. My uncle left the chair there. I was probably in eighth grade or a freshman in high school. I don't know what happened but, that was a time in my life when I had arousing desires with girls.

I remember Cletus and Robert (Jap) would always tease me about Charletta because she liked me. She was a very skinny girl, and people always teased her. I pretended not to like her, but I really did. I found out later that she was LA's cousin. LA was going with my older cousin, Pat. I remember having crushes on other girls, but I always knew I was gay.

Ronnie Smith

CHAPTER 3

1968 – 1971

Aunt Honnie & Uncle Sam

After my uncle, GaGa left us, there were no real male role models in my life. My Aunt Maud liked to drink plenty of beer. Before my uncle left, Aunt Maud would often walk through the house, cursing at my uncle even when he had customers in his barbershop. I guess she acquired an alcohol addiction, which I believe was due to her broken heart. Uncle GaGa moved in with a younger woman, Caroline. She lived in the Austin area, located on the West Side. I very seldom saw him again, but we stayed in touch with no animosity between us. I managed to hold down both of my jobs at Pete's Grocery Store and Red Goose Shoes, and that got me financially through high school.

I spent my last year of high school at Robert A. Waller High School now called Lincoln Park High School. We would have talent shows there, and Big Will and his brother would always sing. There were lots of great talent at the shows. Going to the suburban drive-in was also one of our special treats. We would pile in the station wagon with our treats. Taking your own treats was always cheaper

I don't remember much about either of my graduations. I don't recall what family members were at my graduation. Somewhere between the ages of 14 and 16 years old, my cousin, Diane, lived down the street from me while attending Waller. She lived with the Truss Family, and her boyfriend was Jerome. Our families were kind of close. Diane's friend Irma also lived with them.

I spent lots of my time hanging out with them, especially at Geraldine's house. She stayed on the first floor. She became a good friend and drinking partner. She took me under her wing because I think she knew I was different, gay. I sort of liked her daughter Shelia but, being homosexual stopped me from pursuing a relationship with her. Actually, at that time, I was bi-sexual.

As time moved forward, I begin to explore my homosexual tendencies. The feelings being held inside of me were ready to be explored. I started hanging at Trotter's Tavern on the corner of Willow and Dayton with Peter. Peter's mom, Jeanette, had three more sisters and two brothers. They all lived on Dayton Street in separate houses. I was always hanging out at one of their homes because they always treated me like family. I didn't have a lot of friends, I think, because of my shyness. I was introverted due to my fear and hiding my sexuality. This led me to be around older people. That's when Jeanette's sister, Pat and I became close, and she sort of adopted me as her son. Her daughters, Tammy and Gwen, still call me their brother. I would eventually move in with them later.

My Aunt Maud continued to drink beer and became angrier. I began to take care of myself and worked more at Pete's. This was a big help for me, so I wouldn't have to bother her for money, school supplies, or clothing. That was the beginning of my working career. I've worked consistently ever since then, except for a few years in my life. There was a time when I'd hang on the corner with Bear, Raymond, Pat's brother, and Gene became one of my best friends.

I give 100% applause, love, and credit to my family and extended family for their acceptance and understanding of me and repeated reminders that "you know who you are!"

There are a few exceptions. Those who may have been too "old school," but no love lost on my part. It's God's job to judge us all and not mine.

Ronnie Smith

CHAPTER 4

1971 – 1974

"And the third day there was a marriage in Cana of Galilee; and the mother of Jesus was there: And both Jesus was called, and his disciples, to the marriage. And when they wanted wine, the mother of Jesus saith unto him, They have no wine…Jesus saith unto them, Fill the water pots with water. And they filled them up to the brim. And he saith unto them, Draw out now, and bear unto the governor of the feast. And they bare it…When the ruler of the feast had tasted the water that was made wine, and knew not whence it was…This beginning of miracles did Jesus in Cana of Galilee, and manifested forth his glory; and his disciples believed on him."
John 2:1-3,7-9a,11 King James Version (KJV)

Ronnie Smith

I'm still a little confused about my experiences on Bissell and Willow Street. I know it was around the time when I started working both jobs at Pete's Grocery Store and Red Goose Shoes and went to prom with Brenda. She later gave me her graduation picture and wrote on the back, *"To the guy that took me to prom and had a miserable time."*

I had to agree with her. I really didn't know exactly why but, I think it was because I didn't expect her to wear a wig. Her brother being our escort and driver, didn't make me comfortable either. Although I did know he was coming with us. Or maybe I was just uncomfortable because of my own sexuality? I will confess, it was also about the time I began exploring my sexual attraction and experiences with men.

I will admit, I had several experiences around the time I was 14 to 16 years old. There were a few guys I started seeing during those years, Larry, Michael, Neil, Charles. Sadly, all of them are deceased now. While living on Willow & Bissell streets,

Gene, Bear, and I would hang around Bear's girlfriend Tootie's house near the bar on the corner.

I remember moving in with my Aunt Honnie on the West Side because my Aunt Maud drank heavily and sometimes took her anger out on me. Her attacks made me more introverted, and I spent more time alone, taking long walks at night. During those walks, I'd seek friends, possibly someone that matched my homosexual nature.

On the weekends, I'd take the train to visit my mom on the South Side. My mom lived with different men off and on, including one named Joe. Mom and Joe were both heavy drinkers, and he'd physically abuse her and sometimes me so I couldn't stay with them.

I continued to live with my aunt and cousins on the West Side. Some years later, Aunt Maud moved into a nursing home on the South Side. It wasn't a good place for her and I didn't know why they moved her there. I visited her a few times. She died in 1980 of old age and I believe neglect on the part of the nursing home staff.

After high school graduation, I was working at the Census Bureau. Then Lake Chemical Company on the West Side. Joe later died. My mom lived on 38th and Indiana.

Around 1974 I moved in with my mom before she had my sister in 1975. Things were good for me. A chance to be with my mom again. I was very happy. This was after I graduated from high school and began my working career.

This was an important part of becoming a young independent homosexual man with a newfound freedom. I applied to take the Post Office test for employment. I did pass the test and was called in sometime in 1973. The job was called an N.T.E, meaning "Not to Exceed" a period of 90 days. That actually was the beginning of my Postal career. I was overjoyed even though it was a temporary position, and it lasted for two years. Then they called me for a permanent position as a Mail Carrier. That did not work too well for me with the cold weather and deep snow. I also wasn't good at driving the trucks with the steering wheel on the right-hand side of the truck.

I resigned from that position and asked for my name to be put on the list for a Clerk position. After a few months, they called me back for a Clerk position. That was the highlight of my life. I had to learn and memorize all areas of the city, including all the different zip codes, to properly distribute the mail to be dispersed to the specific mail carrier for delivery. This was very difficult for me to learn, and it took a lot of studying. All this had to be done before you officially got the job.

We were tested once a year. I successfully passed my first one, and had to learn the Hyde Park area on the South Side of the city Eventually, I was assigned to the Lincoln Park area, on the North Side, where I grew up. It made it easier for me because I was familiar with the street names while sorting the mail, but the job was still very stressful. Mainly because it also involved learning the boundaries of all the city's zip codes.

I had several jobs with the Postal Service. It was a joy to be with my mom in Hyde Park. I was especially happy for my mom. She didn't have to live with domestic abuse anymore. I remember my Godmother Pat moved to the South Side too.

I had a new little sister, Monique. Something I always wanted because my other sister Barbara Smith (Babs) had died. I didn't know her, I saw her once. My mom would take care of Monique until I got off of work. While I was sleeping, my mom would often quietly sneak my baby sister into my bed. This gave my mom the chance to sneak off to enjoy her day by continuing drinking or whatever she did outside of our apartment. Who really knows?

I bought the furniture and painted the whole house. I was determined to make us the home I always wanted. A home and traditional family for us. I was ecstatic, making plenty of money and had real, trustworthy friends. I had always been a fearful shy person that lacked self-esteem. Now I could breathe and relax because I finally found comfort in my homosexual lifestyle. This is where I had my first party on 38th and Indiana. This was the only party I've ever had even until today. I remember that it was just a wonderful feeling. My dating life bloomed while living with my mom.

The experiences of my life in my 20s happened at the beginning of my postal career. I worked the midnight shift in the beginning. This career lasted for the next 40 years of my life. I was beginning to feel a bit of happiness after so many years of loneliness. I had my mom, and she understood me and accepted my lifestyle. Besides being my mom, she was a faithful friend that I still miss.

I know that my mom had one sister, Velma, and one brother, who was named Johnnie Smith, Jr., named after my grandfather. They were born and raised in Oak Grove, Louisiana, and grew up living with my great grandmother, Polly Smith. I only remember seeing her a few times, while we went on vacation with my aunt Maud and when I went to my big sister, Babs', funeral. I had only seen her once in my life. She lived in

Ronnie Smith

Colorado with her dad. I was about seven or eight years old at her funeral.

I never knew my mother's mom, Queen Smith. She died when my mom was quite young. My mom told me she was about ten years old when her mom passed. My grandfather, Johnnie Smith Sr. wasn't around until my teenage years. He had been in jail for several years, then later married my step-grandmother, Bernie Smith. We called her Big Mamma. My cousins and I felt our grandfather was a mean and strict man. He was very dark-skinned and never smiled much. I don't know why exactly, but we used to hide from him when he came to visit. I was always the one to get caught, and he would take me home with them for the weekend. It really wasn't so bad. During these weekends, I got to know them better.

Ronnie Smith

CHAPTER 5

1974-1980

Ronnie Smith
Robert A. Waller High School
Class of 1971

Ronnie Smith

I believe growing up without parents played a significant role in many of the decisions I made throughout my life. I had uncles and aunts to guide me a little bit but, never my real parents around me. Their absence made my worry and fear increase as I matured. I think about how people can and cannot influence you sometimes. People can be negative and positive influences. Growing up with or without particular family members affected my development, my mental stability, and how I became a man.

Reflecting on my childhood, I recognize that when you don't have people to really guide you, things tend to go in a bad direction. Without having positive guidance, I was often drawn to negative people. Negative people led me to destructive behaviors and situations that left me stagnant and in the same spot. I felt that with some people, some relatives who kind of kept me in that same spot as an insecure homosexual man. I know I remember being like that since I was 5 years old.

I remember Aunt Honnie telling me something like, "All you gotta do is face reality."

"Ok, explain that to me?" I asked, curious to know what she meant.

She never responded. I think at that point had she just explained that to me, like in a mother-son manner that would have made me grow into a more secure person. I would have caught myself from making future mistakes but, that was the way I see my family on my mother's side. They were the only side I really knew. There were lots of times when some didn't show love for the other person or care about their problems. There was some concern, but they didn't know how to show it to the other person. Often times, the other person might have gained from it and grown. Instead, their concern or love always came with a negative attitude.

Actually, there was some concern, but perhaps I was just different, no judgement and not forcing my spirituality on others.

Ronnie Smith

They would just look at you and ask with sarcasm, "Oh, don't you know better???"

It was always empty answers and those kinds of reactions with the older members of my family. They always responded like that instead of sitting somebody down and explaining what they meant. That goes for my father too. I remember when I was trying to move, I asked him if he could help me. He gave this little crazy look and acted like I wasn't talking loud enough. I knew he just really didn't want to help me move my stuff to the storage and bring it upstairs. I could see him out the side of my eye.

He never really gave me any guidance. In my opinion, this was the best chance for him to stop and give me a talk. You know a father to son talk. Over those years, I made some terrible decisions, and his advice would have been helpful and appreciated. I just lost my furniture due to my overuse of drugs and alcohol. He experienced the same things, in a kind of way but, no, he was thriving despite his mistakes. As for me, I didn't know any better because I didn't have him or anyone else to teach me. That *really* impacted me, and that stayed on my mind for years.

It was the same thing with my aunt. I thought about that for years because I did not understand why they didn't come to me and talk to me? It just caused more and more confusion. There was also my oldest cousin Pat and Linda my other cousin. I found out that they both really loved me, but they didn't know how to show it. Certain things come back to my mind about my cousin Pat. When I was little and how she would say, "Go home and tell your momma to give you some food and stop eating our food."

Later Linda and I worked on the same floor for a few years. I felt that that she somehow ignored me, possibly ashamed, because I wasn't taking care of myself very well. She would jokingly express some negative criticism. I realize now that I took it the wrong way. This is my confession to her and God asking for her forgiveness. May she Rest in Peace in Heaven. They later both became much more loving and caring.

After high school graduation in 1971, I lived with my Aunt Honnie. I was still on the West Side, where they moved from the North Side into a very beautiful home on Quincy Street. It was a big house with lots of rooms. At that time, I was also living with my mom on 39th and Indiana and her boyfriend Joe, who later died of a heart attack. I knew I could live with my mom all the time, but I didn't want to because Joe was abusive and would beat my mom and me sometimes.

I was working at Lake Chemical Company on the West Side near Pulaski and Lake Street. I was very happy because I had to start paying rent to my aunt. It was an excellent job and not really hard work. I was working in the Mail and Supply room mail sorting and preparing orders to be shipped out. All the people were very kind to me except this one lady. Her name was Mary, and she seemed to have some type of attitude problem or a chip on her shoulder. She was quite mean and would physically threaten me.

One time while we were working, she threatened to hit me with one of the scales in the mailroom. It became uncomfortable and unpleasant to work there, but I refused to let her spoil my blessing. I hung in there and continued working at the company. Some months following, my mother's boyfriend died, and things between Mary and I changed. Somehow discussing his death and funeral, I learned his service was at her church. Her attitude changed, and just by having that conversation, Mary became nicer.

Although I was the youngest person in the department, my only concern was being financially stable. I worked overtime whenever it was offered. I made enough money to get my own place. Well, it was actually just a sleeping room. There were a small bathroom and an area with a microwave. My new home was on Wayne Street, near the Red Line. It was perfect, and made it easy to get to work. I had my own place on the North Side of

Chicago without my eight or nine cousins, aunt, and uncle in a really nice neighborhood with restaurants everywhere.

I stayed at my apartment on Wayne Street for about a year, then I moved to another apartment, a larger more modern studio in the Lakeview area. Still on the North Side at 606 Cornelia (Boystown, one of the major gay neighborhoods of Chicago). It was a new freedom for me at 20 years old with a good job and branching out on my own with some peace and happiness.

I had about four new friends from my job. We were really close, but Steve was my best friend. Actually, there were two girls and three guys. We were sort of a party group, with Steve having a car, a Mustang. I think it was red, and we would travel around the city. I think the girls were trying to catch a boyfriend. We would party and drink alcohol sometimes. I remember Kathy trying to get me to have sex with her, but it never happened. Although I was bi-sexual, I was not ready for that.

We all remained friends for a few years. We eventually split-up and went our separate ways or just weren't called back to work at the Post Office because of the ninety-day employment period. Steve and I remained friends much longer. I believe he was fired then later died.

My sister Monique was born in 1975. I was about 19 years old. I had moved back and forth to my mom's house and my own apartment to help her during her pregnancy. I was so proud to have a sister. I was promoted to a permanent employee at the postal service. I was better able to care for them and myself. I was able to move into several beautiful apartments in the Lakeview area.

1976-1980

I had a few other friends by now. There was Keith, we were friends for many years. He later came to visit me in Texas and, we would go to lots of gay bars and ended up having some of the same friends. We eventually parted for some silly reason involving some money. Leonard also lived in the neighborhood. There was Ricky, who was also assigned to the same workstation.

He was probably one of the first guys that I thought I loved. Well, only loved in my mind. He turned out to be a drug addict. He was eventually fired from the Post Office. I dated his brother later, and he had a similar situation with drugs. Ricky and I became very close friends. We would go to breakfast after work, or my mom would fix breakfast for us. This was during a later time when I moved back in with her. I eventually would move back to the North Side.

Things were still going well; I was doing a lot of dating during these years. This was when I began to have roommates living with me. Reflecting back, I feel that wasn't a good thing to do. There was always some type of misunderstanding, or I would end up losing significant portions of my money. I don't advise young gay guys to have roommates if they can help it. This was a point in my life when I was becoming very promiscuous. Often times, I'd either pick up guys at bars, bathhouses, or just on the street. I have also learned that it was not a good idea and was more dangerous than I expected. I found myself in situations where I went to guys' homes and was drugged and beaten.

Although all things were not pleasant, I would say living at 620 Addison was one of my better experiences. I was happy and meeting more people in the neighborhood and at work. We would often go to a bar called Broadway Limited. We, being Charles, Veda, and a few others, and we became close over the years. I later dated Charles.

Ronnie Smith

CHAPTER 6

1980 – 1985

I first thought of moving to Texas after my mom's death in March of 1978. I was feeling a tremendous amount of grief. I believe it was because of the love, hurt, and dysfunctional past that I had with her and my siblings. All this plus my insecurities growing up as a homosexual in a world of shame and unacceptance only added to weakened self-esteem as well as other issues. This is what created an unconscious fear and worry inside me. Not long after my mom's death, I began to spiral into depression, drugs, and alcohol. Aunt Maud also passed away in May of 1980.

I saw several therapists and took a few out-patient classes for depression. One day I was leaving my apartment and saw my Godmother. She asked me if I wanted to come to her house to live. I agreed and stayed with her for about two years on 67th and Merrill in the South Shore neighborhood. I had known her and her family for many years from the North Side while I was growing up. I felt God had sent her as my angel because I had already quit my job at the Post Office.

Most would say I was crazy, but God knew I made the best decision. My Godmother taught me how to build up my concentration and how to relax. This was one of the happiest times in my life. I wasn't feeling so lost and confused. I even spent a month in Montreal, Canada, after I received my first unemployment check.

At this time, I'd like to elaborate on my thoughts and feelings on my arrival in Texas. I felt like I had a brand new chance at life, a breath of fresh air, and a sense of total freedom. It was like a free spirit that was absent during so many years of mostly self-inflicted fear, worry, and confusion, all due to a lack of understanding what true self-esteem and self-love were. I finally had a touch of joy and peace when I arrived in Texas, and my new adventures began. I wanted to find a place to start a new life. A place to start over.

Ronnie Smith

    I decided to call my brother Grady Smith and ask if I could stay with him while searching for a job and saving to get my own place. After all, he knew the stress I was going through after our mom died. We had the same mother but different fathers. I last saw him earlier when we were kids and I traveled to Louisiana where he lived with our oldest sister, Babs, who died at an early age. She died of some type of leukemia. Grady was born in Louisiana and I in Chicago, so we never lived together before this time, but in our younger years, we communicated by writing letters.

    Earlier, when our mom died, I invited him to stay in my apartment on West Cornelia Street. I had a one-bedroom apartment then, and my co-worker Leonard volunteered to pick up my brother and his wife from the airport. I was very nervous and stressed out, having had a hard time driving the car I had rented for their convenience. I also borrowed furniture from a close friend, Mary Belle, who went to high school with me. Grady became very upset and wanted to stay someplace else. I let my friend drive him to where he wanted to go. That was very hurtful but quickly forgotten because we never discussed it again.

He agreed for me to come, but I didn't feel welcome by him as a brother.

After arriving at his place in Texas, there was very little conversation between us. Instead, I spent more time with his sister-in-law Leal and his five-year-old daughter. I took my typewriter with me in hopes of improving my typing skills to gain employment. He stopped me several times from practicing because his father-in-law, who also lived there, was sleeping.

The last straw was when he took money from my drawer. I had received my first week's paycheck for working a temp job, and I was devastated that he didn't even give me a chance to pay him or discuss what I would pay. I did drink some of his whiskey. Perhaps that's why he took the money. I'll never know, but he was angry with my mom for leaving him down South.

Grady was close to my mom's brother Johnnie Smith Jr. who was named after our grandfather but the family called him

Ronnie Smith

Sonny Boy. Unfortunately, Uncle Sonny and I never became close until now. Grady died years later of COPD (Chronic Obstructive Pulmonary Disease) with a lot of anger toward our mother and myself but Uncle Sonny is still alive and about 90 years old but we never communicated until now. He, Grady and my grandfather were ashamed and disapproving of my homosexual lifestyle.

Maybe they all felt it was their right to judge me for being gay. Maybe they felt at fault or blamed each other for me becoming gay. To this day, neither has ever been verbally expressed. Their opinions about my lifestyle and even their silence are part of the time and society in which they came up. I just continue to pray for Uncle Sonny and to love him as my mother taught me to love everyone.

In any case, I had enough, and it was time to get out of Grady's house! I discussed the matter with a co-worker, Margaret, and we both decided the best place for me to go was the YMCA. She helped me move, but unfortunately, things didn't work as I expected. I didn't know we weren't allowed to have overnight guests. I learned this rule when I invited a guy over that I met in a bar. I went to the bathroom and locked myself out of my room by accident. He was heavily intoxicated and ended up falling asleep. The manager let me in, discovered my guest knocked out in my room, and I was asked to leave the next day. I spent a few nights at a bathhouse for men. This was my first time being homeless, it was quite frightening.

I was able to keep my job and go to work each day. Margaret had another suggestion and took me to a place that rented rooms. This place was just outside of the downtown Houston area. It was an old sort of complex that rented to many poor Mexican people. I moved in and thanked God because I didn't have to walk the streets anymore. I was also thankful for my job even though it was temporary. A co-worker, Brenda, offered to pick me up each morning and bring me home each day from work. My temp job was on Westheimer, a street that ran the entire length of the city.

Ronnie Smith

After working as a temp for a few months, I was eventually hired as a full-time employee of the Permian Corporation of Texas, a subsidiary of Oxydental Petroleum Company of Texas. This brought me so much joy. It was a relief from living with the uncertainty of where to sleep from day to day.

My mind started to wonder about how to get out of the roach-infested room. I began to look for my own apartment. I found several places and moved into Mariner Apartments, which was located in the southwest area of Houston. Unfortunately, I didn't have enough money to move in. I called my brother to ask for a loan, but he said no. I took his refusal hard and broke down for a little bit. My co-worker and manager noticed something was wrong with me. After talking to them about what was bothering me, they ended up taking a monetary collection without telling me. When I got to work the next day they gave me enough money and bags of food so I could move. I was in awe and amazement! I was so blessed and grateful that people I barely knew donated and willingly helped me.

I moved into my new apartment a few days later. My co-worker, Carla, gave me a bed and a couch which her boyfriend and his friends brought to me. The apartment building was designed like a cruise ship. It was unbelievably beautiful and affordable for 1980. It had several pools that were needed because of the muggy Houston heat.

Everything I needed was on Westheimer Street, my room, the new apartment, my job, and a gay bar called Midnight Sun. Galleria Mall was located across the street from my job. The mall was gigantic, and I could find anything I needed and wanted. I would go there often to shop or just relax. I began to meet people living in or around my "cruise ship" apartment complex.

The first people I met were transvestites as we called them back then. Charles (Danielle), Jimmy (Peaches), and Isaac (Champagne) took to me quickly, but I felt as if I'd known them for years. Each of them accepted me as their new best friend and were very protective of me. They adopted me as their brother, sister, and best friend. There was a natural comfort when I was with them in their apartment. Peaches liked to visit my apartment when I was cooking. She loved my food, especially my black-eyed peas and curry chicken. They never made any sexual advances toward me. However, I did meet several men through them and dated Peaches' brother Roland for a while.

How my brother treated me at the time didn't matter in light of my newfound family. I learned that God will send us through trials and tribulations for a reason and a purpose. He wants us to see or at least try to understand His Will for us. That experience brought me peace in my life which I would never have understood otherwise. Psalms 23 and 27, my mom's favorite scriptures, stayed on my mind and in my spirit during those days.

The only place I knew to meet people was the Midnight Sun. It seemed to be the single gay bar in town, and this was where Danielle performed as several different artists. Peaches performed as Patti LaBelle and Champagne as Dionne Warwick. They were regulars and always had fantastic shows!

Another place where I met people was The Bath House. That was about 39 years ago when I met another best friend, Shawn Foster, who was from Arizona. Shawn's partner was Walter, and they introduced me to Robert. I started dating him, and later we became roommates. I remember being very unhappy in that relationship because Robert acted like a big baby! He always needed more attention than I wanted to give him. Shawn was my partner in crime. We were always in some type of trouble, like staying out all night and drinking. We eventually went our separate ways but, Shawn and I remained friends the longest. He ended up moving back to Arizona.

I met a lot of other people through Danielle, Peaches, and Champagne. There was Reggie, a close friend of Danielle. He was a fashion designer and moved to Chicago a few years after I returned home. We actually lived in the same building for a while in a high rise on South Michigan Avenue near Cermak Street. We later separated, but I can't recall what happened to him.

    I was basically adjusting to my new surroundings and apartment. Having new friends helped me leave the past behind me. I blocked out my family and those old feelings of hurt and anxiety. My first apartment was a one-bedroom on the third floor. That was where I met Shawn and Robert. Before I got my apartment living in that roach-infested room, I met Larry. He actually became my first roommate in Houston. He was a very nice person and very protective of me. He was also a bit conservative and spiritual, nothing like me during those years.

    I was ready to spread my wings and explore opportunities with my new sense of freedom. However, now I do have some regrets that I didn't get to explore what Larry could have offered me. He advised me not to date someone that he knew before we met. I choose him over that person, but I became bored quickly. I felt like I made a big mistake, but only God knows the truth.

I went on with my life, working every day, and associating with my new friends. Going to Midnight Sun, the Bath House, and continuing my promiscuous sexual lifestyle. I ended up moving to a studio apartment on the second floor in the same building to save some money. It was a lovely studio that had a balcony and was large enough for me.

I can admit that my life was not always a bed of roses. Making mistakes and going left when you should go right are a part of the growing process as we live our lives. My point is to learn about and get to know God because he is the only friend you need.

After moving into my new studio, some of my old negative behaviors surfaced again. I met a young man who, I guess you could say, mesmerized me and captured my trust. He talked me into letting him stay in my apartment while I went to work. When I got home, some of my belongings were gone as well as items I was holding for Robert. This caused both a financial and mental set back. I didn't need any more depression or stress in my life.

 Later I met Joe Baptist, a very dark-skinned, Southern guy that was gentle and humble. From the way I described him, you might think there some sexual tension between us, but there wasn't. We became friends, and he needed a roommate due to his financial difficulties. We became roommates in my studio apartment. This brought on stress, and a desire for space and privacy grew. He had lots of brothers, "country boys," that often climbed the balcony and entered my studio. This didn't really bother me too much because they remained respectful towards me.

 At the same time, my friend Reggie was in a living situation with a white guy but would go back to his family's or lover's house (I'm not really sure which one). The guy was looking for a roommate, possibly temporary or maybe permanent. Expressing how I felt at the time about Joe, Reggie suggested I try moving in with this man. I thought about it and decided to do it. I let Joe hold down the studio, and I moved into this guy's home. I quickly learned that he was some kind of nervous, neurotic, and schizophrenic. I called another guy that was staying with Joe at my apartment and asked him to come and get me ASAP. He did, and I quickly got my ass out of there!!

I quickly got my head together and took control of my apartment and Joe was again my roommate. While I was out one night at the Midnight Sun, I met Edward Cary. We had an immediate attraction. He was a friendly, handsome young school teacher from Norfolk, Virginia, looking for a new start in a new place like me. He never talked about his past in Virginia. I think he was banned from teaching there anymore. He never went too in-depth on the situation, and I never asked about it. We both had our own past life that we wanted to erase and keep behind us.

We became closer and started dating. That grew into daily visits, and a few overnight stays. Both of us had similar dysfunctional family backgrounds. He never met his real mother and father but was adopted by parents whom he grew to love very much. Cary lived with a roommate when we met, but he didn't seem happy about his living situation. He enjoyed staying with me so much that he would make a pallet on the floor for sleeping and let Joe have the bed. I knew there was still a lot to learn about each other's personalities and history, but I felt happy and content. I was falling in love.

    We discussed living together and moved to a two-bedroom apartment in the neighboring complex. Living together in our first apartment was great. We began to meet other people together as a couple, enjoyed each other, and often relaxed by swimming in the pool. It was our chance to unwind from our busy workdays.

    Cary had a white Camaro he loved to drive. This gave me more opportunities to explore different areas in the city and also visit many of the malls. Public transportation wasn't the best, and I didn't like driving anymore after a few driving mishaps in Chicago. For example, there was the time I was driving with my pregnant cousin, Brenda. Thinking that the car was in reverse gear when it was actually in drive, we landed on a hill.

There was also a major car accident in Texas while Reggie was driving his partner's car. For some reason, I had to take the wheel while it was raining, and I slid into some other vehicles. His partner had good insurance so he got behind the wheel, and took the blame for the accident. It shook me up so badly that I've never driven again.

Reggie eventually became our third roommate for a while because we had an extra bedroom. Joe remained our friend, and he and Cary bonded quite well. A few of our other close friends were Leonard, Gene, and James. They stand out because they entered my life when my jealousy and insecurities were arising again.

I felt it was time to clear my mind of the negative thoughts, so I enrolled in two computer classes at Houston Community College. They proved to be a great help to me and my sanity. We also began to take weekend trips to Galveston Beach.

After every class, Cary would find a way to surprise me by jumping out of some bushes or popping out of different places. I never knew when he would pop up. I never took the bus to work because Cary always took me to the office or waited for me outside of my job when I got off. At this point, we were happy and easily falling more in love.

My first major medical issue involved hemorrhoid surgery. While living in Houston, Texas, I developed bleeding hemorrhoids. They made my life a LIVING HELL! They put me in unbearable pain day after day. I had no clue what was causing the pain or what the problem was. I assumed it was the side effects of having some rough and painful sex with recent and past partners. I started seeing a chiropractor, but a co-worker made me wonder if the pain came from my dietary issues. She suggested I see a dietician. I did make an appointment because my body was frail and weak, and I figured there had to be some malnutrition involved.

The situation with the bleeding hemorrhoids became worse and more painful as the days went by. The job with Oxydential Petroleum Oil Company as a file clerk required lots of sitting and bending. By the end of one day, I noticed a bloodstain on my chair. I was so embarrassed when I got up and saw the mess. I reached out for help and made an appointment to see a doctor. After I was evaluated, I learned the situation was pretty severe, and having surgery was the only relief offered. I had been at the company long enough to be full time and have medical benefits.

The operation ended up being a success. I remember Cary, coming to the hospital after the surgery. He put a watch on my wrist to show he had been there while the anesthesia was wearing off. With the excellent care of my partner/lover, I recovered easily. It took a month in bed to get back to 100%, so I couldn't go to work. That was one of the scariest and fearful moments of my life. I give all thanks and praise to Jesus Christ for my recovery.

That's also when we met a group of men that were forming Black & White Men Together. It was a national association of black and white men who identified as gay and interracial couples and supported men in these relationships. Although Cary and I were black, we fit right in because half the couples were black, and the other half were black men dating white men. The members were from all over the country. There were lots of learning and fun activities too.

I have to admit, I was not always perfect and faithful. The president of our chapter was a white guy who dated Lee, a black guy. There was an attraction between Lee and me, which remains to this day. I often think of him when I see Michael Ché on Saturday Night Live. Lee would come to my job with lunch sometimes, and we would go to my apartment for an hour to talk and hold each other. Cary often had a desire to pick up a third person from Midnight Sun and invite them to our house. He wanted to have a threesome. This backfired on him a few times because I was the more sexually aggressive partner.

The idea did not go over well with me either because of my jealousy and not wanting to see him with anyone else. As I reflect back, I realize he was also insecure and jealous of me, but at the same time, he did truly love me. Most people we knew found it easier to talk to me. I would see other people outside of our house. Cary was the complete opposite and liked to bring more men to our apartment, mainly when we partied together with someone else. He discovered that I satisfied them sexually in ways that I didn't do for him.

The straw that broke the camel's back was that he began seeing this guy named Tony. He didn't like me and was causing lots of friction between Cary and me as if he wanted Cary all to himself! He never wanted me to be around, so I began spending more time in my room and not socializing with them.

One night, Tony burst into my room and started questioning me about all the pills I had in the bathroom medicine cabinet. Cary had to show him that they were just some vitamins from my chiropractor for my hypoglycemia. They also helped me concentrate, and my nerves had gotten so bad because of my depression and other reasons. I'm guessing Cary had discussed this further with Tony.

Later, I decided to move back to my old apartment building. After about a month away, I got into some trouble with a guy I was seeing. What a horrible choice! He began stalking me and threatening to kill me. I ended up calling Cary and telling him about my situation. We agreed that I should move back to the apartment with him and Tony. The stalker gave up and eventually disappeared.

I became even more unhappy and uncomfortable returning back to a situation that I chose to leave in the first place. I genuinely believe until this day that Cary was my soulmate. He treated me like a king and with much love in the beginning. In my opinion, it began as one of the best relationships I had. My past relationships were stressful and still left me lonely. As for Cary, nothing lasts forever, and our relationship ended due to my jealousy and personal insecurities. Broken-hearted and homesick, I decided to move back home to Chicago.

My message to my readers is to always keep God in the forefront, before any man in your life. Remember, nothing is possible without having sincere faith and belief that Jesus Christ is your Lord and Savior. You must not let any of the deadly sins guide your life and forget about God. That was the learning process of my life. I believe that was God's will for me; to save me and make me into the happy, joyful, and blessed person that I am today. In life, we are continually growing and changing. We must always work to better ourselves and not be afraid of change. It's best to accept any change that God puts in front of you.

Aunt Maud (Martha)

A Tribute to Martha

"Happiness is gone, loneliness sets in she sits, she waits holding her own it is not dark yet for her strength is the light her price for life is heavy her mind and body racing toward strength overriding a destination of inner destruction, her mind is diseased with crippling thoughts of the past never expressed. Carrying the hurt in her heart keeping strong in the belief of her survival but never to release the guilt, she still tries to maintain the image of that independent woman as she once performed well in her role of existence."

Ronnie Smith

Ronnie Smith

CHAPTER 7

1985 – 1990

"And not many days after the younger son gathered all together, and took his journey into a far country, and there wasted his substance with riotous living... And when he came to himself, he said, How many hired servants of my father's have bread enough and to spare, and I perish with hunger! I will arise and go to my father...And he arose, and came to his father... But when he was yet a great way off, his father saw him, and had compassion, and ran, and fell on his neck, and kissed him... But the father said to his servants, Bring forth the best robe, and put it on him; and put a ring on his hand, and shoes on his feet: For this my son was dead, and is alive again; he was lost, and is found. And they began to be merry."

Luke 15:13,17-18a, 20,22,24 King James Version (KJV)

Five years later, on my return to Chicago, it felt good to be home. When I returned from Texas in 1985, I went to Aunt's Honnie's house. It felt good to be back home. I had actually gotten a little homesick. My departure was sad and heartbreaking because of splitting up from my partner, Cary, of three years. I really did love him, and there are so many memories of us together. We lived in beautiful townhouses and apartments, and the weather was always great. I have to admit I was jealous and insecure because he had a lot of admirers, which caused lots of stress and depression for me. A lesson learned, do **not** love anyone more than you love yourself.

Back in Chicago, five years later, I began to work on getting my job back at the post office. After a few months, with some help from my good friend Ginger, I was hired back in my previous position as a clerk, another joyful day for me. After five years, I was quite grateful to be blessed and reinstated in my last job. At that moment, I felt like that prodigal child that God so lovingly accepted back home after going astray. I started working with Ginger in 1973 when I was initially hired.

It was good to see my family too. I hadn't stayed in contact with them since leaving. As I mentioned previously, my mom had died, and I had been full of sadness and anger, only causing destruction to myself. I returned to live with my Aunt Honnie on the West Side off and on.

Being back in Chicago allowed me to reunite with some family members, including my sister, Monique, who was living with my mom's first cousin, Tina and her husband, Frank. I attempted.to stay with them for a while until I got back on my feet. I also wanted to develop a relationship with my sister. Unfortunately, that did not work because it felt like Frank didn't want me to stay there.

I can't remember what was said, but I do remember the room where I slept had rats, and it was hard to sleep in that room. I went to sleep with Monique in her room, and I don't think he liked that. Later, I learned he was molesting my sister. I moved away to my own apartment, but I was unaware of his behavior. I just continued to visit her. This was very heartbreaking for me because I had been away from Monique for so many years. To come back to this type of treatment and being separated from my sister was difficult.

From there, I moved into several apartments on the North Side. After a few months of working, I moved to my own apartment on Grace and Pine Grove. Once I was back in Lakeview, I rented another one bedroom. Then I later moved to a large studio apartment. I believe I was there for a few years. A few things I remember are my ex-partner, Cary, coming to visit me from Texas. He was dating Tony when I left Texas but the relationship didn't last long. We always remained friends, although he did bring his new partner with him. At this time, I was dating Alvin, and we eventually ended up living together, but it was a good reunion. Cary later died in a car accident.

After getting adjusted to being back home, back in that environment, I quickly fell back into some bad habits. I remember being in the apartment, crying and playing lots of music that reminded me of my mom. I got through that with time. Grief is sometimes hard to get past or learn to cope with, but I want others to know it's possible to overcome.

I applied for the Personal Assistant position in Human Resources after working a short while as a mail clerk. Receiving much persuasion and guidance from two of my supervisors, Ms. Carrigan and Ms. Cooksey, I applied for the job. Having learned typing while enrolled at Taylor Business Institute of Chicago gave me the skills needed for the position. I was later chosen for an interview and eventually offered the position. After screaming and jumping up and down with excitement, I called Ms. Lambert from Human Resources back and accepted the job.

I worked the second shift from 3:00 am - 11:00 pm in the Photo ID Unit of the Personnel Services Department, where I took pictures and created replacement photo ID badges. I was also responsible for some light filing and typing. This new job was quite exciting, but I did have to adjust to those quiet evenings. Although I did work the midnight shift for years in the Mail Room, it was never quiet. I did have Johnny, a co-worker that worked in Labor Relations who assisted me at that time. Then I was transferred to the day shift. On those days I got to know some very nice people.

I was trained for the hiring process, beginning with administering the strength and stamina tests for the Mail Handler candidates. Their requirements were to lift bags weighing at least 70 pounds of mail correctly, and I also learned the proper skills to interview for all positions. This new job also included handling transfer requests from other government agencies. My tenure working in Personal Services lasted throughout the 90s.

Many things in my life began to change, including the ending of my two-year relationship with Alvin. We lived in his apartment on 20th and Michigan, so I moved around to several apartments on the North Side. I moved back on Grace and Pine. At one point in time, I remember having my ten year old sister, Monique living with me at the address on Grace and Pine. She had survived abuse from our cousin Tina's husband, gone to a few foster homes and living with her father for a while. With it being difficult to care for her and work, my office manager, Charles Jones, suggested we move out to The Harvey House in Harvey, IL. They had living quarters and help for my sister from the women at the church as well as myself.

I was beginning to drink alcohol a lot. Soon it became uncomfortable for me to live there. They had lots of strict rules and meetings. There was this one guy that was always checking on us randomly. I began to think this was some kind of cult because of all the rules and regulations. It didn't take much time for me to search for apartments back in the city. I found one in the Roger Park area at 1622 W. Sherwin on the North Side again. We quickly moved, and I got guardianship of Monique. Once we moved to Sherwin, one of my family members promised to continue to take my sister on the weekends. That was good for us.

Ronnie Smith

CHAPTER 8

1990-1995

Monique Nicole Smith & Ronnie Smith

Ronnie Smith

Once Monique and I settled in, I had her enrolled in Sullivan High School, and then Lakeview High School. Although she has special needs with her Glaucoma in one eye and being born with Fetal Alcohol Syndrome slowed her down a little bit, she graduated. Eventually, I got her a job, and she worked for the post office for a short while afterwards. Monique worked in Section 6 as part of a special program for employees with disabilities.

This was the beginning of a downfall for me over the next twenty years. Working full time while maintaining our household as a single gay man became difficult. Monique was becoming very unhappy because she was maturing with very little female guidance. I performed my duties at home and on the job quite well for a few years, but as the stress increased, I started drinking again. Being in a dysfunctional relationship with Charles, which lasted for ten years, only increased my drinking and created more arguing and fighting with my sister.

Monique eventually began to rebel against me. Maybe it was because I would not let her hang out the way she wanted. I have always been overprotective of her, but Monique wanted so badly to imitate what she saw me doing. She saw me drinking and having male partners like Charles live with us. Having them live with us took my attention away from her.

At the same time, negative changes in my behavior became obvious to my co-workers and supervisors. I was later demoted and moved to work in Section 6, the Mail Processing Department. This department was across the street in our old building. I was assigned the late shift that started at 11:00 pm and ended at 7:00 am. I processed different types of mail and packages for the Mail Carriers to deliver the next morning. There was a working crew of about eight to ten people. It was a peaceful, quiet atmosphere, but I had to learn to switch my sleeping habits again. I slowly adjusted to the shift and saw it as a blessing. At that time, the department had to downsize the Personnel Services Department. Good thing for me that was another solution for me instead of getting fired. I felt very grateful to still have a job.

After about two years in our old building, our mail sections were moved to the new building across the street on Harrison. My starting time also changed to between 5:00 am and 8:00 am. This caused me travel problems because I had to follow the CTA schedule. Sometimes it would still be dark outside. I would get to work late often or just call off.

Monique witnessed as I suffered through plenty of turmoil with two of my partners, Paul and Charles. Once Charles even stopped my sister from stabbing me. I think at the time she thought her boyfriend was attracted to me. I got rid of all our knives in the house shortly after that. I did all I could to help Monique, which stressed me out. I began drinking more and losing control of my house. Charles moved out but not far away.

Monique met several groups of shady people and got a job in a program for disabled people where I worked. I think these new "friends" were trying to take advantage of her, but she would not listen to me. I began to spend more time at Charles' apartment. While I was gone, they took her money, clothes, everything in Monique's room. I decided to take her and move again. We moved to Charles' building.

1996-2001

This new apartment was not too far away from Sherwin Street. Charles' apartment was on the first floor, and we were on the third floor. Usually, one of us was in the other's apartment, and it felt like we were living together again. This was all happening when I wasn't spending time with my family. They were not there to help with my sister, and we did not live close to them. A lesson to learn here is sometimes you help people too much and lose yourself. Something that I was doing, and it was stressing me.

While I was living in that large drug-infested courtyard building on Fargo Street, Monique moved to her own apartment on the first floor. Special Services and the homeless shelter where she stayed for a few months helped her get an apartment on the first floor. It was a real blessing to have Monique living so close because one day I became very painfully sick in my stomach. It felt like I was being stabbed over and over. The pain was so intense I could barely walk. I crawled from my third-floor apartment to her place on the first floor. I kept ringing Monique's doorbell, but for some reason, she never answered even when I knocked on her door. I knew she had begun using drugs and still associated with more shady people. Perhaps there were other drug users in her apartment, and they didn't want to let me in?

Eventually, an ambulance was called, and I was taken to the emergency room in Evanston Hospital. The first diagnosis was that my intestines were wrapped around my stomach. I never got a clear understanding of how this happened. During the surgery, it was discovered that my appendix was about to burst. A second surgery was required to remove it. Now, I have two odd-looking scars on my stomach. After the second surgery, I was wrapped in a girdle type band around my mid-section. It became very tight after the operation, and I was in excruciating and unbearable pain. I screamed and yelled for help from the intense pain of the uncomfortable wrap. I was told the person that put the band on me was out to lunch. I assumed it was so tight to hold the stitches close and in place to heal correctly. Honestly, this was the worst pain I've ever experienced in my life. I can still remember it until this day.

Previously, Monique met a young man everyone called Dinky and got pregnant. She had a son named Sean, whom I love dearly like he is my own son. Monique and Dinky broke up. I think he was drinking a lot and she didn't like that. She became more rebellious after the break-up. Charles started smoking crack cocaine. With some influence, I started smoking with him. This was the beginning of financial problems, which later led to bankruptcy.

Monique decided she didn't want to live there any longer and wanted to go to a shelter. She took Sean, and they moved to the Corner Stone Shelter in the Uptown area. I was worried about my sister and my nephew. My drug and alcohol use continued and began my dysfunctional behaviors. All our money was being spent on drugs, and I was starting to miss days from work. Another message to learn is drugs and alcohol can lead to a lack of self-esteem and not caring for yourself.

I want to also say that on that same street, Fargo, I was evicted or asked to move because I was behind in my rent payments. I ended up getting an apartment down the street. I put my back rent in the mail slot they had specifically for the rent but, they never got it. I was evicted. I later got the money back and moved back to the first building. A true blessing because I believe and know God recognizes a sincere heart. God gives us chances and forgiveness. It's up to us to continue being righteous or to decide to fall into sin.

In 2001 Charles began to get sick; he was diagnosed with Cancer and some old Air Force injuries, and he eventually died in 2001. After caring for him and going back and forth to the hospital, I suffered some grief, but I did experience some relief from a stressful relationship that lasted about ten years. The only support I had during his funeral was Sean, who was only two years old then. I could feel some stress and resentment from his family because he left me $15,000. They had control of the money, but I did get it later.

Monique was still rebellious and insisted on being on her own. Remember, she had some disabilities. Monique began to meet with shady people that would later take advantage of her and her apartment by moving in, offering her more drugs and blocking me from seeing her or my infant nephew, Sean.

At this point, I became more stressed out with worry about my sister and her son. I took care of him since his birth. My life was quickly getting out of control, and we all needed help. I decided to call the Department of Children's Services. They took my nephew, and one of my cousins got temporary custody of him. My sister went to another cousin's house. I went into a drug and alcohol rehab, Bill Family near Fullerton and Western. It was in a three-story building with a family type atmosphere.

Ronnie Smith

This worked for me for about six to eight months. They intended to teach me to live without drugs and alcohol.

Ronnie Smith

CHAPTER 9

2002-2005

"So Jesus came again into Cana of Galilee, where he made the water wine. And there was a certain nobleman, whose son was sick at Capernaum. When he heard that Jesus was come out of Judaea into Galilee, he went unto him, and besought him that he would come down, and heal his son: for he was at the point of death. Then said Jesus unto him, Except ye see signs and wonders, ye will not believe. The nobleman saith unto him, Sir, come down ere my child die. Jesus saith unto him, Go thy way; thy son liveth. And the man believed the word that Jesus had spoken unto him, and he went his way. And as he was now going down, his servants met him, and told him, saying, Thy son liveth. Then enquired he of them the hour when he began to amend. And they said unto him, Yesterday at the seventh hour the fever left him. So the father knew that it was at the same hour, in the which Jesus said unto him, Thy son liveth: and himself believed, and his whole house. This is again the second miracle that Jesus did, when he was come out of Judaea into Galilee."
John 4:46-54 King James Version (KJV)

After leaving Bill's Family, I managed to get an apartment on the West Side close to my family's house near Congress and Laramie. I was working all the time while in rehab. I was able to move right in and get some furniture. Monique moved in later, and so did George, my roommate from Bill's Family. Our newly found freedom was destroyed, and Satan arrived! We were smoking and drinking again. None of us were actually happy, not understanding each other nor getting along. I think my biggest mistake was letting George move in with Monique and I without really knowing him outside of rehab. While I was working nights, Monique would lock her bedroom door in fear of George, who she thought was a sexual predator. I also began having sex with George and doing more drugs as a result. I always suspected that he was after Monique as well.

I remember talking to Aunt Honnie, and she said I had hit rock bottom. She was the only mom I had at that time. I listened to her and decided to get rid of George. We were fighting a custody case with DCFS (Department of Children & Family Services) against Monique involving Sean's dad, and his mother. That didn't go well, and my sister let them take Sean. She met Rockne in rehab on the West Side, had another baby, and later married him. Currently, they don't have custody of their children today because their drug and alcohol situation has not changed.

    I checked myself into the Salvation Army for rehab in 2005. I was still stumbling through life and trying to find my lost self-esteem and running from my fears. Going to rehab was a much-needed change. After 28 days, lessons, chores, and meetings, there was an expected improvement in my addictive behaviors. I lived in a private room as long as I wanted, and I was expected to return to work. I did that for somewhere between one and two years.

    I qualified for the Family Medical Leave Act benefits with my job due to my previous medical issues. This saved my position and kept me from getting fired. I must confess to misusing that privilege several times because I still had a drinking and drug problem. My job with the post office allowed me 28 days off to go to rehab several times at the Salvation Army.

There was more freedom with the Salvation Army rehab facility compared to the place in Harvey. I could go out anytime, but I had to be back before their curfew. I followed their program because they created and designed it specifically for me. For the most part, I was happy and stayed sober. I did meet a few guys in the program, didn't use good judgement, and became involved with them. I ended up suffering some emotional pain, and hurtful experiences again, mainly financial. I was learning to listen, obey, and surrender when it came to the teachings of God. Another lesson I learned and want to share with others like me is to love yourself more than anyone else except God!

After rehab, I found myself apartment hunting again. I moved to a great studio in Lakeview on 542 W. Melrose St. Again. I was happy and content with my life, and had a chance for a new beginning in Boy's Town, the largest gay community in Chicago. It was a great area to live in, and I fit in perfectly.

There were lots of fabulous stores up and down Broadway Street, and the bar scene was very active and fun. Monique and Rockne would often visit with their new daughter, as well as my nephew Sean, and his grandmother. Life was pretty good.

I was eventually offered and given a later start time at the post office. It helped and I did improve with getting to work, but I was still late sometimes. Thankfully my supervisors often allowed me to make up any time later when I could. God was indeed on my side, and I accepted that blessing in my heart and my mind knowing it was from Jesus. I made several improvements in my life, and I was so much better than before. I owe much gratitude to two managers, in particular, Mr. Sconiers and Mr. Clark.

Ronnie Smith

CHAPTER 10

2005-2007

Ronnie Smith

In 2005, I spent one to two years living at the Salvation Army due to some past drug and alcohol abuse problems in the preceding years. Once again, these actions caused me to hit "rock bottom." This caused a lack of self-love and respect for myself. I became irresponsible and regressed back to the old ways of meeting and inviting people to my new place. This was not so healthy for me, especially after having some "clean" time. I was doing much better and took care of myself by exercising, taking care of my apartment until the loneliness, depression, and lusting for companionship and sex took over. I was off to the races again. Inhaling the rush from the drugs and liquor.

I continued this behavior for several months, smoking cigarettes, crack cocaine, and drinking heavily. It was the grace and mercy of Jesus Christ that kept me living. Regardless of my negative behaviors, I managed to keep my job at the post office. Continuing down that path of self-destruction, I had a heart attack.

Miracles

    I remember how heavy my habit of cigarette smoking was when the heart attack began. I felt very dizzy and lightheaded. Sweat began pouring down my face, and a severe pain in my chest throbbed throughout my entire body. It felt like sharp knives were stabbing the inside of my chest. I was able to call an ambulance for help. They took me to Illinois Masonic Hospital. This was a day that I will never forget. I was immediately admitted to the hospital and diagnosed with a heart attack. They rushed me into surgery and placed a stunt in my heart, which opened my arteries and allowed my blood to continue to flow throughout my body. I was released from the hospital and returned to light duty at work after several weeks of recovery. I went six months to a year sober and not smoking cigarettes, which, I think, contributed the most to the heart attack. I went back to enjoy my beautiful luxurious studio apartment on West Melrose Street near Lake Shore Drive.

    Loneliness and a need for companionship came into play again, and my eyes began to wander with lustful reasons.

Ronnie Smith

I was crossing the street at Belmont and Broadway when I saw Jimmy standing across the street. There was an immediate attraction. During those days in the LGBT or gay community, dating was not the same as dating for heterosexual couples. They would date for maybe two weeks or even months before having sex. In the gay community, all this was done sometimes in one night. Of course, this did cause concern about the possible transmission of sexually transmitted diseases now known as STIs or sexually transmitted infections. This was especially true in light of the HIV/AIDS epidemic of the 1980s.

I am thankful for the many medical advancements that later saved countless lives allowing many people to live healthy and undetectable. I lost so many friends during that time due to a lack of knowledge, proper medication, and medical treatments, which were ineffective in the fight against the disease. This led to careless sexual acts among homosexuals and drug addicts, taking the lives of many. That was the road Jimmy and I took. It led to more self- destruction, and unhappiness for me.

The drugs and alcohol begin again. Leading me back to financial and mental stress and instability. Jimmy later told me he had been to jail, but I don't remember when or why. I never asked, a bad habit of mine. I never got the necessary information from my partners to make wise decisions. As time went on, our relationship became more dysfunctional with drug and alcohol use. I wasted so much money. This seemed to become a habit of mine for all my life.

Jimmy had a history of being a slick user! Many bisexual men just out of jail would come to Boy's Town and prey on homosexual men. I abruptly stopped while we were in the middle of attempting a sexual encounter and he tried to blackmail me because of that. I told him I wanted to wait a bit longer because I had recently gotten over a previous exposure to a STI. Jimmy became a little angry, saying that I should have told him sooner so we could have gotten condoms or some form of protection just in case.

By then my head was distorted and my mind was cloudy. I wasn't thinking clearly, and he took advantage of me. He used this as his reason to start manipulating me. One time he threatened that he would tell the guys I dated that I had a STI. He said he wouldn't tell if I cosigned a car for him. I told him that my credit record was not good, and I would never agree to sign for anything.

Later, I discovered stolen packages from my building's lobby in my living room. These were packages delivered from the post office, and I became extremely nervous and afraid, which caused lots of tension and stress for me. I was still working at the post office and could have lost my job and possibly gotten arrested. After all tampering with mail is a federal offense! That episode of my life ended when I saw a lady with a photo of Jimmy in the lobby. She said he had assaulted her in some way. We came to an end after all that drama and I let him go for good.

I want my readers to learn the importance of self-love. This is so important and needed to get through the challenges and trials that life can bring. They can sometimes be overwhelming but, you can't give it up! Try to develop a true faith in God. A belief that in His time, He will rescue and save you. Not in your will or time but in His. I hadn't learned this yet, and the roller coaster of my life continued.

Several months later, the vicious cycle remained when I met Dwayne. Similar to the previous situations with men, Dwayne and I had a few drinks, and drugs which ended with me having him overnight. A few days became months. I allowed him to get too comfortable and believed his promises to help me out financially. I eventually discovered he was homeless and allowed myself to continue going down the previous path with drugs and alcohol. All of those distractions caused me to lose my grip and mastery of my home. Back-to-back situations like this took quite a toll on my mind and body. I had a heart attack just two years before.

"Wow, what does it take for me to learn?" I asked myself.

Ronnie Smith

I have always had a problem with anxiety and depression, but dealing with Dwayne was the straw that broke the camel's back. My situation had become obvious to the neighbors with all our noise and the smell of drugs. No one said anything to me, but one lady mentioned my behavior to Ed, who I first met in the Salvation Army.

I made up my mind to get help, and I discussed this with Ed. Dwayne and I agreed that I would go back to rehab at the Salvation Army while he stayed in my apartment for one more month. Then I would notify management that I was no longer living there. That was one of the worst mistakes I've ever made. That was a great example of how drugs, stress, and insecurity can affect your thinking. I was never successful reaching out to the apartment management and only managed to leave messages. Later I was notified that Dwayne left my place a mess, and I was sued for $3000 in rent and damages to the property.

I met Ken at the Salvation Army while I was walking down the hallway passing him. As he caught my attention something came to my mind that said DON'T MESS WITH THIS MAN! However, it just happened, and our conversation got me hooked on him. I was struck and that was it, I ended up following old habits again. Our relationship lasted over a period of a year. I got really hurt dealing with him, financially and mentally and experienced lots of loss.

I continued my stay at the Salvation Army rehab facility. By the grace of God, that was my last time staying there. Unfortunately, that was not the last of my bad experiences with drugs and alcohol, but it was a break from my addictions. The next year was much more relaxed, and I was able to cope with the routine created by the rehab at the Salvation Army. I had my own room, but it was like an apartment to me. I was able to come and go as I pleased, but there was a curfew. I was able to keep my job thanks to the understanding of my managers and supervisors.

That was the last time I saw that gigantic red building on West Monroe. No more hiding nor being paranoid because the area was also where many of my coworkers delivered mail. One of the young men who was also in rehab had a sister who was the mail courier for the building. She was also a coworker of mine whose name escapes me. She turned out to be a very comforting, interesting, and understanding person even to this day. Occasionally, I went with her on the route. The rehabilitation center was a safe haven, but sometimes it felt more like a jail than a recovery facility for drug and alcohol addicts.

After my recovery and release, I got my own new apartment and once again had a total sense of freedom and less tension. I had the freedom to make my own rules, and I felt blessed to have another chance to leave my hectic pass behind. I had to get new furniture for my bedroom, kitchen, and living room. The only thing I remember having was my suitcase full of memories from my mom, awards, books, and a television. I also had my CD player and a few clothes. It didn't really matter because I was so grateful that God gave me another chance. Through his grace and mercy, I was able to establish a meaningful life with self-esteem and self-confidence.

Miracles

No more rehab, but I did move into another apartment at 1040 Hollywood in the Edgewater neighborhood. I had such a hard time getting this place because of my credit and past evictions. It was a blessing from God that I got it. By that time, I had learned that God does not want us to misuse our blessings. I was relearning and practicing that once again and experiencing full-blown joy and happiness. I was still blessed with my good job after a full year of being clean and sober when life took another turn.

Ronnie Smith

CHAPTER 11

2007-2013

"The Lord shall cause thine enemies that rise up against thee to be smitten before thy face: they shall come out against thee one way, and flee before thee seven ways."
Deuteronomy 28:7 King James Version (KJV)

Ronnie Smith

    I began to get lonely and started looking for companionship. On one summer night, I was taking a walk downtown when I met Curtis. He was a bit younger than me, and he was actually homeless. Curtis lived in and out of shelters or stayed with friends. We began to have a sexual relationship. Our relationship grew, and he ended up staying with me every night. He even got a temporary job. We grew closer, and I developed trust in him. One day he was in the washroom, and I began to wonder why he was in there for so long. I opened the door, and Curtis was in there smoking a crack pipe. I didn't resist and asked him to give me some. I think he was trying to respect me and not indulge around me, but it didn't work. I was off to the races again.

    This went on for a few years. Somewhere around 2007 to 2009, I faced more financial problems, and I was also jeopardizing my job and home. I knew I needed to seek help. After going through a few AA meetings and therapy, I was introduced to the Howard Brown Clinic. They had different types of classes for young gay men that wanted to change their lives and behaviors. While there, I ran into Terry, a person I previously met at a similar organization. He was looking for a roommate, and I accepted due to my financial situation. The drug use and promiscuous sexual activities continued. I quickly began to feel the roller coaster that I road previously. I was worried that I was about to start up something terrible again. Depression and confusion were entering my life again.

    Terry began to show strange behavior like wanting me to believe he was seeing shadows on the walls or hearing noises that never happened. His sister once asked, "How do you do it?" She was giving me a message about putting up with him. Terry's daughter came to visit on the weekends. She looked at me and did a circular motion above her head, implying that he was crazy, but I ignored those signs at first. Then one day, I went to get in the bed and, Terry had a sword lying on the bed. I asked him why it was on the bed. I forgot what Terry said, but he removed it quickly. It was in a case, as a souvenir. After that, no more was said about it.

I actually met Terry a few years ago at a clinic. He asked me for my number as if he was interested in being friends or dating. We exchanged numbers, and when he did call, he said it was an accident and never called again. I was a little hurt because it felt as if Terry was playing games with me. I told myself to never talk to him again if I happened to see him. The message here is to follow your first mind. When you meet strangers and feel a negative vibe in your mind or heart, I suggest to just leave them alone.

I came home from work one day and thought someone had broken in and robbed me. Many items were missing but, Terry had actually moved out and took my possessions when he moved! Once again, I found myself facing eviction with shame and very low self-esteem. I called my friend Ed who helped me put some personal items into storage, and I arranged to move in with a lady from church.

She seemed to have some mental issues. She would scream at me each morning to hurry and leave the house. My storage was in her name, and she failed to make a payment after I gave her the money. Also, she and Terry had become friends. I felt like they were plotting behind my back because they had several phone conversations and meetings.

I began to feel very uncomfortable in her home, so I left her house and moved in with Ed. He offered me a deal, but I could only be there like every other day. I would not be able to do that, but we did live together once before. Luckily, I met one of his friends, Mark, who invited me to move into his place for a week or until I could get a room at the men's club around the corner from his house. When I checked my debit card, I didn't have enough money because I trusted Ed to get money off my card for drugs and alcohol.

We were partying, and I wasn't in my right mind at the time. I was devastated, lost, and confused about what I was going to do. Also, Mark had to leave for about a week to help his parents in Rochelle, IL. There wasn't even a chance to stay there for that week. I contacted my cousin Brenda, who told me that another cousin Darrell wanted me to call him. I did, and he agreed to let me stay with him. In my mind, I was thinking maybe I'd stay with him for a few weeks or a month while working to get my own place. I believe Darrell and his mother thought I was planning to stay longer because he needed help to pay his rent and maintain his apartment, but Mark returned, and I went back to his house.

    I felt like my family was a little disappointed and I thought Darrell did not believe I was coming back to pay him. Darrell's mother said I couldn't come back if Mark didn't let me stay with him. I'm sure she didn't mean any harm, just tough love. I could tell Darrell was surprised when I returned with the money by the look on his face. I know if I stayed there, my aunt wouldn't have to help him as much, but that just wasn't my plan. I went back to Mark's studio on Leland Street near Broadway on the North Side of Chicago. Weeks turned into months and then years of me staying there. I had to sign-in to enter the building, so I would visit other people and then go to his place to keep a low profile.

Eventually, the apartment's management caught on, but they didn't bother me. Instead, they agreed that I could stay until I found a place or applied for an apartment in the building. Mark eventually learned of rumors about me circulating from the haters and backstabbers in the building and my visits to other residents before coming to his place in my efforts to hide that I was staying with him. Mark spoke to the management on my behalf, and by that time, I was familiar with the desk clerks and began to just walk in without signing in.

This went on for three years. Again, I found myself engaged in old destructive behaviors, like smoking crack cocaine, abusing alcohol, and partaking in promiscuous sexual activities. This only caused me more stress and anxiety, and I was unable to save enough money to move. Another eviction was hanging over my head, and I felt forced to be in a relationship that I was completely unhappy with. I was living in a small studio, sleeping in a twin bed with another person. We weren't always in agreement with each other, but felt forced to go along.

We didn't buy much food, but Mark cooked basic meals like chicken breast and vegetables from a can. The best thing for us was our neighbor Rosie who cooked for us just about every other day. She was a blessing and reminded me of a godmother or an aunt and later took to me like a mom would. We became friends, and she was a big help to me and provided positive guidance. I was with Rosie when she last went to the hospital and passed away. May she rest in peace.

Mark and I were still in the Leland Building, which had lots of studio apartments, a few one-bedrooms on the top floor, and two stories were some kind of harm reduction drug in house program where people with drug or mental issues lived. Levels two and three were regular unsupervised apartments, but the entire building was drug-infested and didn't help with my own problems.

It was 2011 when I found myself having some shortness of breath and chest pains. After smoking crack cocaine, cigarettes, and drinking heavily, I found myself at Weiss Hospital. I felt disgusted and angry because my habits had me in the hospital. I was eventually admitted, and the breathing problem was under control. I was feeling better, the x-rays were done, and some lymph nodes were found on my lungs. I was advised to see my Primary Care Physician who sent me to Kellogg Cancer Center at North Shore Evanston Hospital. This is where the doctors diagnosed me with lung cancer. After a complete examination, the doctor decided to do surgery and remove one-third of my right lung.

To this day, I am doing fine and cancer-free. Thanks to the blessings and the grace of God, it was caught early. After a month of healing, I quit cigarettes after spending 30 years smoking them. I did resume smoking crack for a few years after that, but there is no smoking of anything today.

Ronnie Smith

I managed to retire from my job in January 2013. My 30-year employment at the post office was long and hard, but also a real blessing at the same time. I was grateful and thankful to God for sending some of his most awesome angels to guide, teach, and help me to get to where I am today. I'm especially grateful to those coworkers, supervisors, and managers at the post office who cared, criticized, and pushed me to get through all my trials and tribulations. I thank Jesus Christ for each of them.

Soon after, Mark got a call from his parents in Rochelle, asking him to come home, and stay with them because they both were ill. He decided to go and left me to care for the apartment. The residents were familiar with me, and the new desk clerks thought I was Mark. I thought to myself, living here alone could be a chance for me to get my life together and change the negative behaviors. I wanted to build up my health, get fit, and have peace of mind. It wasn't easy and didn't happen overnight. I actually spent another year continuing the things Mark and I practiced, but began to get tired, and he was still trying to have control over me from far away. Like checking on me and not wanting me to have company. By the second year, I realized I had to do something to change my life for the better.

Ronnie Smith

CHAPTER 12

2013 to the Present

"After this there was a feast of the Jews; and Jesus went up to Jerusalem. Now there is at Jerusalem by the sheep market a pool, which is called in the Hebrew tongue Bethesda, having five porches. In these lay a great multitude of impotent folk, of blind, halt, withered, waiting for the moving of the water. For an angel went down at a certain season into the pool, and troubled the water: whosoever then first after the troubling of the water stepped in was made whole of whatsoever disease he had. And a certain man was there, which had an infirmity thirty and eight years. When Jesus saw him lie, and knew that he had been now a long time in that case, he saith unto him, Wilt thou be made whole? The impotent man answered him, Sir, I have no man, when the water is troubled, to put me into the pool: but while I am coming, another steppeth down before me. Jesus saith unto him, Rise, take up thy bed, and walk. And immediately the man was made whole, and took up his bed, and walked: and on the same day was the sabbath… The man departed, and told the Jews that it was Jesus, which had made him whole."

John 5:1-9, 15 King James Version (KJV)

My work on this memoir has allowed me to reflect on a number of things. The different paths I might have taken over the years, the many people in my life, and my own insecurities. I've especially been thinking a lot about my homosexual lifestyle and the other gay men I encountered one way or the other. One lesson I've been learning all of this time is discernment when it comes to people in general, but more importantly when it comes to the men with whom I had relationships.

I counted four or five men, who caused the most friction in my life, but as you've read, there have been many others who effected my life positively or negatively. As I bring this trip down memory lane to a close, I'm reminded of more. For example, there was also Reggie, an older man who knew my mom. He and I met in a bar and began a sexual relationship back in 1977, which led to me moving in with him. That decision, like so many afterward, was a complete disaster, but I won't go into the details here. The most important thing to know is that I've learned

Reggie, and all the others weren't entirely the problem. On the one hand, I chose them because I lusted for them physically, but my insecurities and the resulting poor judgment were always the real problems. At the same time, many of those men most likely saw my vulnerabilities as well as an opportunity to take advantage of me.

This pattern, while obvious to me, now was only just beginning to become clear to me during the years I spent living alone in Mark's place. Despite all of the warnings and advice from so many well-meaning people in my life not to get involved with those shady, suspicious characters, I had to learn for myself. Now I understand and accept that I had to make my own choices in order to learn some harsh but important life lessons. Without a doubt, the most important thing I've gained is the knowledge that God, in the form of the Holy Spirit, was interceding and attempting to lead me. Those experiences, as well as the words and teachings of my mother, were what lead me to focus more on my spiritual life and my relationship with God.

I got involved with my church, attending Bible Study. One of the men there took me under his wing like a mentor providing some tough love without any games, deceptions, or attempts to take advantage of me and my insecurities. This proved to be very helpful to me. I'd always been in and out of churches since I was a little boy. By that time, I began to concentrate more on learning the teachings of God, and I knew a Holy Spirit was guiding me.

That decision lead to several positive changes in my life. I began to save money a little at a time, eventually stopped smoking crack and cigarettes, but still drank occasionally and became more involved with my family. In February of 2016, I moved out of Mark's place into my current apartment at last, and the feeling was GREAT! A large eighth-floor studio with beautiful hardwood floors and twelve windows on two sides giving me a perfect view of Lake Shore Drive and Lake Michigan to the East and the rest of the city on the West. When I walk outside in the summer, I can feel the refreshing Chicago wind blowing. Finally, my mind and body had a sense of calm. A true blessing from God despite many health concerns which I still deal with today.

Towards the end of 2017 my kidneys began to fail, and I signed up for the transplant list at Northwestern Hospital. In the meantime, I endured dialysis treatments three days a week for six months. While the machine removed, cleaned, and cycled my blood back into my body, it left me feeling weak for a short time, but it was a tremendous help. I was also suffering from a fractured vertebra and ribs in my back and chest, respectively, during three months of that waiting period.

Shortly after returning from a family reunion, I got a call from one of the nurses at Northwestern Hospital that a kidney was available for me. It was being flown in from New York, and I had to be at the hospital at 12:00 am that night, or should I say *morning*? I remember being so overwhelmed by the tears rolling down my face that I had to pass the phone to my friend Mark to speak for me.

Ronnie Smith

After being on dialysis for six months, I had a kidney transplant despite a tremendous amount of fear on July 30, 2018. Although I had surgeries before, that one frightened the heck out of me! I remember the Operating Room and looking over to see the doctor wetting the kidney. I can't even describe what I felt at that time. I guess I was in shock. Especially when they gave me the anesthesia by pressing a gas mask heavily onto my face. It felt like someone was trying to choke me to death until I was unconscious.

I remained in the hospital for about four days, and afterward, the pain was unbearable without medication, so they gave me morphine and some other pain reliever. I also remember one of my cousins came to see me. She worked in the hospital and saw me having a panic attack. It was so embarrassing, I felt like something was going wrong. My bell for the nurse wasn't working correctly. I couldn't use the bathroom, and I was scared.

After four days, I was sent home with very specific instructions about cleanliness, especially for my hands. I had a total of 18 pills to take twice a day and a stent in my penis with a long tube connected to a bag to collect and measure my urine every hour. My blood pressure, and temperature, were also taken every hour. I had the most gigantic and painful staples in my stomach and was relieved when they and the stent were finally removed.

This went on from four to six months with multiple trips to the hospital, and several follow up appointments for the next two years. I was also treated for a Background Virus (BK virus) that was causing my body to reject the new kidney. I was told that one out of every eight kidney transplant patients has this problem, but I am now in stable condition and have been for a couple years. There have been a lot of total lifestyle changes, but they have all been for the better. I can do and eat lots of things that I couldn't before. I just can't get carried away. It takes lots of patience and concentration not to overdo it. It is just like having a full-time job. Yet, God is good all the time, and I am healed! Another prayer answered. Another miracle received. To all those non-believers, my advice is to accept Jesus as your Lord and Savior, believe with your whole heart, and watch your prayers get answered.

Now in my 60's I do kind of wish I had a baby, whether on purpose or accidental. However, the only time I think about this is when I get lonely. I think about not having an immediate family around me about 90% of the time. I hardly ever talk to my cousins on the phone, and I miss my brother, sister, and mom. I sometimes even miss my dad. I think of them and what it would have been like to be a real family.

These thoughts bring loneliness and an empty void in my spirit. Then I think, maybe having a child or a grandchild would fill some of that void. That's the only reason I believe I feel a desire for a child. I don't think God really meant for me to have them. I prefer to just go on and be happy with myself. To pursue real goals and happiness with myself and maybe a partner. I really miss having a partner, but I know that God's going to bring one to me. I know that's something God wants me to have, and I really believe He will supply that.

Thinking back over all the ups and downs, mistakes and lessons, trials and miracles, things lost and things gained I am reminded of one final scripture, which has brought me comfort over the years. One last piece of advice for my readers who are still learning, growing and trying to live a better life.

"Wait on the Lord: be of good courage, and he shall strengthen thine heart: wait, I say, on the Lord."

Psalm 27:14 King James Version (KJV)

Ronnie Smith

A Living Miracle and a Prodigal Child of God

Ronnie Smith

TESTIMONY

My name is Ronnie Smith. I am a saved Christian, I do believe in Jesus Christ, and I believe that he is my Lord and Savior.

When I began to write my testimony, I wondered if saved/Christian was the correct way to describe myself. I decided yes because I know that some higher power brought me through all the trials and tribulations in my life that I had overcome. I came to know and believe that higher power was Jesus Christ. Before learning the story of the Bible, I would refer to Him only as God. Now I understand that God and Jesus Christ are one.

I am saying Christian because I have always carried in my heart a desire to be a God-fearing person and a righteous man even through my trials and tribulations. I was faithful as well, even when I was sinning. I am not perfect even now, but I am much better than before.

Ronnie Smith

I am a witness to God's forgiveness and mercy. Coming from a life of a dysfunctional childhood causing insecurity and low self-esteem and lots of fear and very little family guidance. I am grateful to Jesus Christ for delivering me from a life of years of alcohol and drug use. Through years of fear and confusion, he delivered me from and got me through several chronic health illnesses that could have taken my life.

I survived a heart attack in 2005 with having a stent put in my heart. In 2011 I developed lung cancer after smoking for 30 years that also included drugs, cocaine for five years.
A few years ago, I developed kidney disease. That put me on dialysis at the beginning of 2018. In Jan of that year, my kidneys failed, so I was on dialysis for six months.

That July, I got a call from Northwestern Hospital, letting me know that they had a kidney for me. I was on the list for the past year and a half. Some people wait much longer or never get one. Truly a blessing. So I give praise and Glory to Jesus Christ, my Lord, and Savior.

Thank You

Ronnie Smith

Ronnie Smith

READER REVIEWS

Ronnie,
I enjoyed reading the first few chapters of your book, and could certainly relate. I'm sure anyone struggling with low self-esteem, fears, hidden or open sexual identity will be able to benefit greatly from it.

Good Luck to you!
Your friend Babs

I have had the pleasure of reading his adaptation of the events of his life. I've read the correspondence and have found it to be a trip down memory lane. Of course, I was not aware of many of the events that occurred, and my heart was quite heavy. However, I think he has displayed a tremendous amount of courage to revisit these incidents as well as publicizing such. As I stated before, Ronnie is a trooper!! I sincerely hope if the reader is experiencing similar tribulations he/she would receive his message of defiance to succumb to negative energy and find strength in Ronnie's story to overcome the roadblocks that are/were placed before them.
I sincerely pray for Ronnie's absolute success in this endeavor as well as any future projects he decides to conquer!!

Thank you,
Tammy Yance

I love how he introduced each character and their significance. I also identified with how each of these people helped to make his family unit. Growing up an African American kid in a dysfunctional family everybody we encountered was important to us. I could feel the loneliness within from Ronnie and how he never wanted anyone else to feel that pain. He searched for love and carried God with him as he continued to accommodate everyone in his path to freedom of the mind, peace. I love you Ronnie excellent read.

Your Big Sis-friend for life and supporter,
JoAnn Clay

Miracles: A Prodigal Child of God addresses the themes of abandonment, resilience, and defiant joy. I have been blessed to pastor Ronnie over the past few years. It has been wonderful to be a part of his unfolding story, but what is even more joy-inducing is that he is now sharing that story with the world. Ronnie is a survivor and from his pain and triumph, we can find principles and practices that can promote healing, aid us in accomplishing our dreams, and help us discover that God is always willing to embrace God's children--particularly the prodigal ones.

Rev. Jamie Frazier,
Founder & Lead Pastor, Lighthouse Church UCC